GETTING TO KNOW THE WORLD'S GREATEST ARTISTS

MICHELANGELO

WRITTEN AND ILLUSTRATED BY MIKE VENEZIA

CONSULTANT MEG MOSS

CHILDRENS PRESS ®
CHICAGO

For Jeannine

Cover: Detail of *David*. 1501-1504.
Marble, 16 feet, 10 inches.
Galleria della Accademia, Florence.
Scala/Art Resource, New York

Library of Congress Cataloging-in-Publication Data

Venezia, Mike.
  Michelangelo / by Mike Venezia.
      p.   cm. — (Getting to know the world's greatest
artists)
  Summary: Describes the life of the Italian Renaissance
artist and examines some of his paintings and sculptures.
  ISBN 0-516-02293-8
  1. Michelangelo Buonarroti, 1475-1564—Juvenile
literature. 2. Artists—Italy—Biography—Juvenile
literature. [1. Michelangelo Buonarroti, 1475-
1564. 2. Artists. 3. Painting, Italian. 4. Painting,
Renaissance—Italy. 5. Art
appreciation.] I. Title. II. Series.
N6923.B9V44   1991
700'.92—dc20   91-555
[B]   CIP
[92]   AC

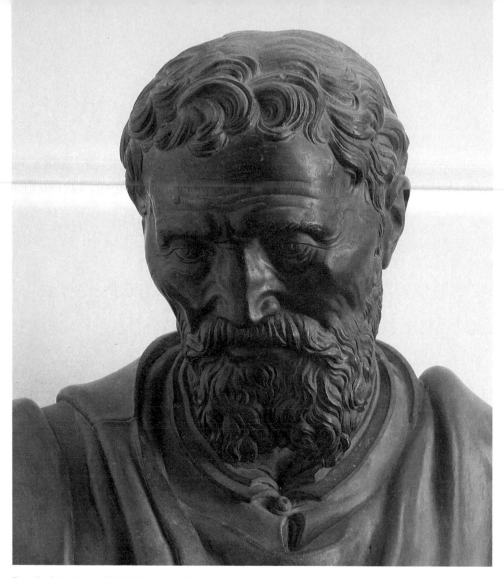

Detail of the *Bust of Michelangelo*. By Danielo da Volterra. Bronze.
Galleria della Accademia, Florence. Scala/Art Resource, New York

Michelangelo Buonarroti was born
near Florence, Italy, in 1475, during
a time known as the Renaissance.
Many people think he was the
greatest artist who ever lived.

Michelangelo was a master of architecture, painting, and poetry. But his favorite art was making statues of people.

Michelangelo sculpted many of his statues from big blocks of marble. He chipped away at the marble with a hammer and chisel, until he got it the way he liked.

The unfinished statue of *Saint Matthew* shows how Michelangelo started one of his statues.

Saint Matthew. c. 1506. Marble, 8 feet, 11 inches.
Galleria della Accademia, Florence. Scala/Art Resource, New York

Michelangelo
made his statues
look very lifelike.
Sometimes he
would polish them
so they looked
smooth and shiny.

6

Detail of
The Medici Madonna.
1524-1534. Marble,
7 feet, 5⅜ inches.
Medici Chapel in
the New Sacristy
of San Lorenzo,
Florence.
Scala/Art Resource,
New York

But sometimes Michelangelo would leave chisel marks. The marks helped give his statues shape and a feeling of being alive when they were viewed from a distance.

When Michelangelo was born his mother may have been too ill to take care of him. His father took him to live with a family of stonecutters.

When he grew up, Michelangelo joked that this was the reason he loved to cut away at stone so much.

Michelangelo lived in just the right
place and at just the right time. In the
1400s and 1500s, people in Florence
were very interested in architecture,
painting, poetry, and sculpture.

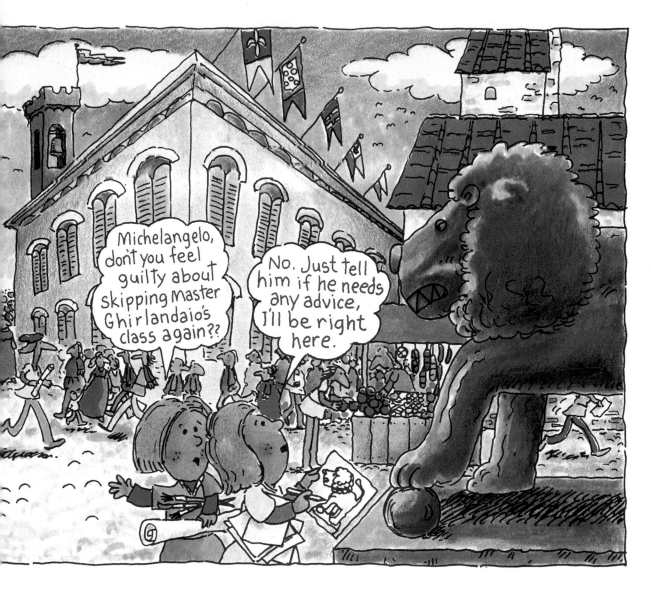

When Michelangelo was 13, he learned a lot about art by just walking through the streets of Florence on his way to the school and workshop of Florence's most popular artist, Domenico Ghirlandaio.

The Ascension of St. John. By Giotto, from a fresco cycle of the Life of St. John the Evangelist. Peruzzi Chapel in Santa Croce, Florence. Scala/Art Resource, New York

Michelangelo loved the paintings of Giotto and Masaccio that he saw on the walls of churches in Florence,

Payment of the Tribute by Christ. 1425-1428. By Masaccio, from a fresco cycle of the Life of St. Peter. Brancacci Chapel in the Church of Santa Maria del Carmine, Florence. SuperStock, New York

Left: *St. Mark.* 1411. By Donatello. Marble, 7 feet, 9 inches.
Church of Orsanmichele, Florence. Scala/Art Resource, New York

Right: *Story of Abraham.* 1425-1452. By Ghiberti, gilt bronze panels,
31¼ inches. East doors of the Florence Baptistery, right side,
2nd field, Florence. Scala/Art Resource, New York

and he admired the sculptures of
Donatello and Ghiberti. These artists
lived and worked in Florence before
Michelangelo was born.

Michelangelo learned a lot on his own, but he also learned many things about being an artist from his master, Ghirlandaio.

One important thing that Ghirlandaio may have taught Michelangelo was the difficult art of fresco painting. To make a fresco, an artist paints on wet plaster. As the plaster dries, the painting becomes part of the wall and lasts a very long time. This is because the paint won't flake off.

Fresco painting came in very handy for Michelangelo later on, when he began his most famous painting, the ceiling of the Sistine Chapel.

Michelangelo's first love was sculpture. When he was about 16, he went to study at a new school that was only for sculptors. It was started by the wealthiest and most powerful man in Florence, Lorenzo de' Medici. Lorenzo loved art of all kinds and paid artists to create works of art for him. People who paid artists in this way were known as patrons.

Lorenzo soon realized that Michelangelo had a special talent and invited him to live at his palace. The sculpture on the next page was one of the first Michelangelo did at Lorenzo's school.

Michelangelo studied as hard as he could to become a good sculptor. But it wasn't until he visited Rome that Michelangelo showed people how good he really was.

Rome was another great art city in Italy. Michelangelo made a statue for a wealthy patron there that amazed everyone who saw it.

The *Pietà* was so beautiful, people found it hard to believe it was done by such a young artist. Michelangelo was only 24.

Pietà. 1498-1499. Marble, 5 feet, 9 inches. St. Peter's Church, Vatican City, Rome, Italy

The people who ran the city of Florence heard about Michelangelo's beautiful statue. As soon as he returned home, they asked him to carve a statue for Florence. They even gave Michelangelo a huge block of marble to work with. Michelangelo was very happy. He couldn't wait to start.

It's all yours Michelangelo.

Think of it as a present.

Gee, thanks everyone!

THIS END UP

Michelangelo turned the block of marble into his most famous sculpture. The statue shows David ready to fight the giant Goliath. But *David* also shows that the people of Florence thought of themselves as strong, brave, clever, and ready to defend their city.

During this time, the powerful ruler of the church in Rome heard about Michelangelo. Pope Julius II wanted to build beautiful churches and statues in Rome so that people would remember him. He asked Michelangelo to come there to work. At first, everything was fine. Pope Julius wanted Michelangelo to carve a group of statues for him. But soon after Michelangelo started, Julius lost interest in the project. He decided there was a much more important job he wanted done.

Julius asked Michelangelo to paint the large ceiling of the Sistine Chapel. Michelangelo was disappointed. He told the pope he was a sculptor, not a painter. Pope Julius didn't care what Michelangelo thought and practically forced him to begin painting. During the time it took to paint the ceiling, the pope and Michelangelo had many arguments.

Ceiling of the Sistine Chapel. 1508-1512. Vatican Palace,
Vatican City, Rome. Scala/Art Resource, New York

After four years, Michelangelo
finished the ceiling.

It turned out to be one of the most
wonderful paintings in the history of art.

Creation of Adam. Detail from the Sistine Chapel ceiling.
1510. Fresco, 110 ⅛ x 224⅔ inches.
Sistine Chapel, Vatican Palace, Vatican City, Rome. Scala/Art Resource, New York

Michelangelo painted many scenes
from the Bible. One of the most famous
scenes shows God giving life to Adam.
The looks on the faces of God and
Adam and the realistic way

Michelangelo painted their bodies
had never been seen in a painting
before. Suddenly, Michelangelo
became known as one of the greatest
painters in the world!

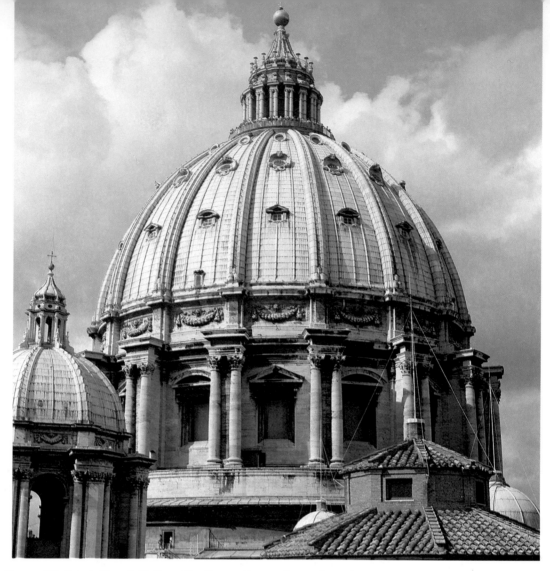

Dome of St. Peter's Church, Vatican City, Rome. Gaetano Barone/SuperStock, New York

After the Sistine Chapel ceiling was finished, Michelangelo went on to create many other beautiful and important works of art, including plans for building the famous dome on top of St. Peter's Basilica in Rome.

One of the things that made Michelangelo such a great artist was his ability to give a *special* energy and strength to the people he painted and sculpted. Even though the statue of Moses is sitting very still, Michelangelo was able to give him a feeling of great power

Moses. Detail of the Tomb of Julius II. 1506-1513. Marble, 8 feet, 4 inches. San Pietro in Vincoli, Rome. Scala/Art Resource, New York

Michelangelo lived to be nearly 89 years old. He was working on a sculpture called the *Rondanini Pietà* just a few days before he died.

Detail of *The Rondanini Pietà*.
c. 1552-1564. Marble, 6 feet, 3⅝ inches.
Castello Sforzesco, Milan.
Scala/Art Resource, New York

Below: *Creation of the Stars and Planets.*
Detail from the Sistine Chapel ceiling.
1511. Fresco, 110⅕ x 224⅖ inches.
Sistine Chapel, Vatican Palace, Vatican City, Rome.
Scala/Art Resource, New York

Michelangelo felt the human body was the most important subject an artist could paint or sculpt.

Detail of the *Last Judgment*. c. 1536-1541. Fresco, 48 x 44 feet.
Sistine Chapel (altar wall), Vatican Palace, Vatican City, Rome. Scala/Art Resource, New York

He spent much of his life studying nature and science in order to make his works of art as lifelike as possible.

Recently, Michelangelo's paintings in the Sistine Chapel were cleaned. When years of grime were removed, people were surprised to find that Michelangelo used much more color in his paintings than could be seen before.

The works of art in this book came from the churches and museums listed below.

Casa Buonarroti, Florence, Italy
Castello Sforzesco, Milan, Italy
Baptistery, Florence, Italy
Galleria della Accademia, Florence, Italy
Notre Dame, Bruges, Belgium
Orsanmichele, Florence, Italy
San Lorenzo, Florence, Italy
San Pietro in Vincoli, Rome, Italy
Saint Peter's Basilica, Rome, Italy
Santa Croce, Florence, Italy
Santa Maria del Carmine, Florence, Italy
Vatican Palace, Rome, Italy